Abraham Lincoln

Abraham Lincoln

James M. McPherson

OXFORD
UNIVERSITY PRESS
2009

OXFORD
UNIVERSITY PRESS

Oxford University Press, Inc., publishes works that further
Oxford University's objective of excellence
in research, scholarship, and education.

Oxford   New York
Auckland   Cape Town   Dar es Salaam   Hong Kong   Karachi
Kuala Lumpur   Madrid   Melbourne   Mexico City   Nairobi
New Delhi   Shanghai   Taipei   Toronto

With offices in
Argentina   Austria   Brazil   Chile   Czech Republic   France   Greece
Guatemala   Hungary   Italy   Japan   Poland   Portugal   Singapore
South Korea   Switzerland   Thailand   Turkey   Ukraine   Vietnam

Published by Oxford University Press, Inc.
198 Madison Avenue, New York, NY 10016
www.oup.com

The Library of Congress Cataloging-in-Publication Data
McPherson, James M.
Abraham Lincoln / James M. McPherson.
p.   cm.   Includes bibliographical references.
ISBN 978-0-19-537452-0
1. Lincoln, Abraham, 1809–1865.
2. Presidents—United States—Biography.
I. Title.
E457.M46 2009
973.7092—dc22
[B]
2008035623

Frontispiece: Courtesy of the Library of Congress Prints and Photographs Division. Photographed
by Anthony Berger at the Brady Gallery, Washington, D.C., February 9, 1864.

Endpapers: Draft of the Gettysburg Address, November 1863. Courtesy of
the Library of Congress Manuscript Division, Washington, D.C.

3 5 7 9 8 6 4 2
Printed in the United States of America
on acid-free paper

To the memory of

Donald H. McPherson

1945–2008

Vietnam War veteran

FBI agent

Civil War buff

and winemaker extraordinaire

Contents

Preface

During my first year in graduate school at Johns Hopkins University in Baltimore, a local radio station telephoned the Department of History to ask if it could recommend someone to answer questions about Abraham Lincoln from listeners to a call-in show scheduled for Lincoln's birthday, February 12, 1959. I had recently completed a research paper on Lincoln's secretary of war, Edwin M. Stanton, so the department suggested me. Being young and foolish, I took on the task. It was a sobering learning experience. What I mainly learned was how much I did *not* know about Abraham Lincoln.

In the half century since that day, I have learned a great deal about Abraham Lincoln, but I continue to encounter new information and new insights. My own perspective has also changed during that half century. I wrote my doctoral dissertation, which became my first book, on the abolitionists during the Civil War and Reconstruction. Like many young historians, I tended to adopt the viewpoints and attitudes of the people about whom I was writing. Most abolitionists were sharply critical of Lincoln in the early years of the Civil War for what they perceived as his slowness to move against slavery and his apparent deference to the border states and Northern conservatives on questions of emancipation and race relations. Lincoln never fully caught up with the abolitionist and radical Republican positions on these questions, and my own attitudes reflected their continuing criticisms of him.

Only after years of studying the powerful crosscurrents of political and military pressures on Lincoln did I come to appreciate the skill with which he steered between the numerous shoals of conservatism and radicalism, free states and slave states, abolitionists, Republicans, Democrats, and border-state Unionists to maintain a steady course that brought the nation to victory—and the abolition of slavery—in the end. If he had moved decisively against slavery in the war's first year, as radicals pressed him to do, he might well have fractured his war coalition, driven border-state Unionists over to the Confederacy, lost the war, and witnessed the survival of slavery for at least another generation.

I have written a lot about Abraham Lincoln in my career. Others have written more. During this bicentennial commemoration of his birth, a large number of excellent biographies and other books about Lincoln have appeared and continue to appear. Most of these are substantial works; one definitive multivolume biography runs well over a half million words. Amid this cascade of information, I believe there is room for a brief biography that captures the essential events and meaning of Lincoln's life without oversimplification or overgeneralization. This is what I have tried to do in the following pages.

J. M. M.

Abraham Lincoln

Abraham Lincoln was born on February 12, 1809, in Hardin County, Kentucky, about fifty miles south of Louisville. His father, Thomas Lincoln, had come as a child with his family from Virginia in 1782. Thomas acquired only enough literacy to sign his name but gained modest prosperity as a carpenter and farmer on the Kentucky frontier. He married Nancy Hanks, also illiterate, in 1806.

Abraham was born in a log cabin on Sinking Spring Farm three miles south of Hodgenville. When he was two years old the family moved to another farm on Knob Creek about seven miles northeast of Hodgenville. On this farm of 230 acres (only thirty of which were tillable), young Abraham lived for five years, helped his parents with chores, and learned his ABCs by attending school for a few weeks with his older sister, Sarah.

In December 1816 the Lincolns moved again, this time to Indiana, which had just been admitted to the Union as a state. The traditional notion that the Lincolns moved because of a dislike of slavery may have some truth; they belonged to a Baptist denomination that broke from the parent church on the slavery issue. The main reason for the move, however, was the uncertainty of land titles in Kentucky, which caused Thomas to lose much of his property. Indiana offered secure titles surveyed under the Northwest Ordinance. There Abraham learned the use of axe and plow as he helped his father carve a house and farm out of the hardwood forest. The growing youth also snatched a few more months of education in the typical one-room schoolhouses of the frontier. In late 1817 or early 1818 the Lincolns were joined by Nancy's aunt Elizabeth Hanks Sparrow and her husband, Thomas Sparrow, and Abraham's cousin Dennis Hanks. Soon thereafter, in the fall of 1818 the Sparrows and Nancy Hanks Lincoln all died of "milk sick," probably caused by drinking the milk of cows that had grazed on poisonous white snakeroot.

After a year of trying to keep house and raise the children by himself, Thomas Lincoln returned to Kentucky to seek a wife. On December 2, 1819, he married the widow Sarah Bush Johnston and brought her and her three children to his farm on Pigeon Creek, Indiana. His stepmother provided Abraham with affection and guidance. With a desire for learning and an ambition for self-improvement, he devoured every book he could borrow from the meager libraries of friends and neighbors. The King James Bible and *Pilgrim's Progress* offered him maxims for life as well as a model for the poetic prose that characterized the best of his later writings. Thomas Lincoln neither encouraged nor understood his son's intellectual ambition; quite the contrary, he chastised Abraham's "lazy" preference for reading over working.

The teenaged Abraham's thinly veiled disdain for the life of a backwoods farmer doubtless irritated his father. Abraham in turn resented the requirement of law and custom that any wages he earned before he reached the age of twenty-one—by hiring out to neighbors to split rails, for example—must be turned over to his father. Abraham Lincoln's hatred of slavery, which denied to slaves the "fruits of their labor," may have been influenced by Thomas Lincoln's expropriation of Abraham's earnings. In any event, relations between Abraham and his father grew increasingly strained. When Thomas lay dying in January 1851, he sent word that he wanted to say goodbye to his son. Abraham refused to make the eighty-mile trip, stating that "If we could meet now, it is doubtful whether it would not be more painful than pleasant."[1] He did not attend his father's funeral.

In 1828 Lincoln and a friend took a flatboat loaded with farm produce down the Ohio and Mississippi rivers to New Orleans. He repeated the experience in 1831. These trips widened his horizons and, according to popular belief, shocked him with the sight of men and women being bought and sold in the slave markets of New Orleans. Recalling another trip on the Ohio River to Louisville, he wrote years later that "there were, on board, ten or a dozen slaves, shackled together with irons. That sight was a continual torment to me; and I see something like it every time I touch the Ohio, or any other slave-border."[2]

Although Abraham came of age in 1830, he did not strike out on his own. Once more his father sold the farm and set forth to greener pastures, this time in central Illinois. After helping his father clear land, Abraham hired out to split rails for other farmers—and this time he kept his earnings. In the summer of 1831 he settled in New Salem, a village on the Sangamon River bluff about twenty miles northwest of Springfield.

Lincoln's six years in New Salem were a formative period. For a time he drifted from one job to another: store clerk, mill hand, partner in a general store that failed, postmaster, surveyor. His partner in the general store drank up all the profits and then died. Although Lincoln was required by law to repay only his half share of the debts left by the store's failure, he insisted on repaying all creditors in full. He wryly referred to this burden as his "national debt," but he also earned a valuable reputation as "honest Abe," a nickname that would stick.

Six feet four inches tall, with a lanky, rawboned look, unruly coarse black hair, large ears, a gregarious personality, and a penchant for telling humorous stories, Lincoln made many friends. Among them were Jack Armstrong and his gang of young toughs, "the Clary Grove boys." As the new kid in town with a reputation for physical strength, Lincoln had to prove his mettle in a wrestling match with Armstrong, who had previously beaten all challengers. Sources disagree on who won the match— apparently it was a draw—but Lincoln won the respect and loyalty of Armstrong and his friends despite his refusal to participate in their drinking and hell-raising.

In 1832 the Sac and Fox Indians under Chief Black Hawk returned to their ancestral homeland in Illinois, precipitating the short-lived Black Hawk War. Lincoln volunteered for the militia and was elected captain of his company, which included the Clary Grove boys. They saw no action, but Lincoln later recalled his election as captain as the most gratifying honor of his life. But he also mocked his own military experience in a later speech on the floor of the national House of Representatives, when as a congressman he opposed the Mexican War. "Did you know I am a military hero?" he asked the Speaker of the House. "I fought, bled, and came away" after "charges upon the wild onions" and "a good many bloody struggles with the Musquetoes."[3]

Another side of Lincoln's complex personality was a deeply reflective, almost brooding quality that sometimes descended into serious depression. Lincoln described this condition as "the hypo," for hypochondria, as medical science then termed it. This recurring ailment, coupled with Lincoln's almost morbid fondness for William Knox's lugubrious poem "Mortality" (1824) and his later self-reported dreams in which death figured prominently, may have resulted from the deaths of loved ones: his mother, his sister Sarah in childbirth in 1828, and Ann Rutledge seven years later. Lincoln met Ann Rutledge at her father's tavern in New Salem, where he boarded in 1833. Their story has taken on so many layers of myth and antimyth that the truth is difficult to determine. For half a century, until the 1990s, professional historians discounted the notion of their love and engagement, but new scholarship has revived the credibility of a Lincoln-Rutledge romance, and biographers now accept its reality. Ann Rutledge died in August 1835, probably of typhoid fever, and Lincoln suffered a prolonged spell of "hypo" after her death.

During the New Salem years Lincoln developed new purpose and direction. The local schoolmaster, the aptly named Mentor Graham, guided his study of mathematics and literature. Lincoln joined a debating society, and he acquired a lifelong love of William Shakespeare and Robert Burns. He also acquired a passion for politics and in 1832 announced his candidacy for the legislature. Although he failed to win the election, he received 92 percent of the votes in the New Salem district, where he was known. When he ran again in 1834 he campaigned throughout the county and won decisively.

Lincoln was a Whig and a devotee of Henry Clay, whom he described as his "beau ideal of a statesman." Clay's American System, with its emphasis on government support for education, internal improvements, banking, economic legislation to promote growth and opportunity, and a tariff to protect American industries, attracted him. In the legislature Lincoln came under the wing of John T. Stuart, a Springfield attorney and Whig minority leader in the house. Stuart encouraged Lincoln to study law and guided him through Sir William Blackstone's *Commentaries on the Laws of England* (1765–69) as well as other books whose mastery was necessary to pass the bar examination in those days. The encouragement worked. On September 9, 1836, Lincoln obtained his license to practice law. In 1837 he moved to Springfield and became Stuart's partner.

Lincoln won reelection to the legislature in 1836, 1838, and 1840, going on to become floor leader of the Whigs and a prominent member of the "Long Nine," Whig legislators from Sangamon County who averaged more than six feet in height. Legislative logrolling enabled the Long Nine to get the state capital moved from Vandalia to Springfield (more centrally located) in 1837. During the same session, Lincoln and one colleague from Sangamon County entered a protest against a resolution passed overwhelmingly by the legislature that denounced antislavery societies in such a way as to imply approval of slavery. Declaring human bondage to be "founded on both injustice and bad policy," Lincoln and his colleague nevertheless criticized the abolitionists, whose doctrines tended "rather to increase than to abate [slavery's] evils."[4]

Although ill at ease with women, Lincoln in 1836 began a half-hearted courtship of Mary Owens, whose sister lived in New Salem. A year later she broke off the relationship, to the probable relief of both parties. In 1839 Lincoln met Mary Todd, who had come from Kentucky to live with her married sister in Springfield. Despite the contrast between the educated, cultured, and socially prominent daughter of a Lexington banker and the socially awkward, rough-hewn son of an illiterate farmer, Mary and Abraham fell in love and became engaged in 1840.

What happened next remains uncertain and has been the subject of much speculation and debate among biographers. Lincoln seems to have developed doubts about his fitness for marriage and broke the engagement. He may have become infatuated with another young woman who visited Springfield that year, Matilda Edwards. It is even possible that a rivalry for Edwards's affections developed between Lincoln and his best friend, Joshua Speed. Whatever took place, it seemed to have reached some sort of climax on New Year's Day 1841—a day that Lincoln later referred to as "that fatal first of Jany. '41."[5] Lincoln plunged into an even deeper depression than had followed Ann Rutledge's death. Three weeks after that "fatal first of Jany." he wrote that "if what I feel were equally distributed to the whole human family, there would not be one cheerful face on the earth."[6] He told Joshua Speed that he would be "more than willing to die" except "that he had done nothing to make any human being remember that he had lived."[7]

Lincoln's depression may have stemmed from feelings of guilt about his treatment of Mary Todd. He would be happy enough, he wrote to Joshua Speed in 1842, were it not "for the never-absent idea, that there is *one* still unhappy whom I have contributed to make so. That still kills my soul. I can not but reproach myself, for even wishing to be happy while she is otherwise."[8] Soon after writing this letter, Lincoln resumed his courtship of Mary Todd. Speed had married in 1842, and his assurance that matrimony was not so frightening after all seems to have encouraged a conflicted Lincoln. On November 4, 1842, he and Mary were wed in her sister's home.

The quality of their marriage has been much debated among historians. It produced four sons—the first, Robert, was born exactly nine months after their marriage. Mary shared Abraham's lively interest in public affairs. He often sought her advice and she encouraged his political ambition. In personality, however, they were in many ways opposites. He was disorganized, careless in dress, and indifferent to social niceties; she was quick-tempered, sometimes shrewish, dressed expensively, and lived by the strict decorum of Victorian conventions. He got along with almost everybody; she quarreled with servants, workmen, merchants, and some of Lincoln's friends. He was absent from home on the legal or political circuit for weeks at a time, leaving her to cope with the trials of household management and child rearing. His moodiness sometimes clashed with her fits of temper. Over time her mental stability became more fragile. Recent scholarship suggests that she may have suffered from bipolar disorder.[9]

After retiring from the state legislature in 1841, Lincoln devoted most of his time to his law practice. The same year he formed a new partnership with Stephen T. Logan, who helped him become more thorough and meticulous in preparing his cases. The Springfield courts sat only a few weeks a year, requiring Lincoln and other lawyers to ride the circuit of county courts throughout central Illinois for several months each spring and fall. Most of his cases involved damage to crops by foraging livestock, property disputes, debts, and assault and battery, with an occasional murder trial to liven interest. Lincoln was especially effective with juries. His homespun humor and ability to explain legal issues in colloquial language gave him an edge with the laymen who made up these juries. Lincoln also had a knack for focusing on the main issue in a trial and conceding nonessential points to his adversary, lulling him into complacency. "But giving away six points and carrying the seventh he carried his case...the whole case hanging on the seventh," wrote a fellow lawyer. "Any man who took Lincoln for a simple-minded man would wind up with his back in a ditch."[10] By the time of his marriage Lincoln was earning $1,200 a year, income equal to the governor's salary. In 1844 he bought a house in Springfield—the only home he ever owned. He also dissolved his partnership with Logan and formed a new one with twenty-six-year-old William H. Herndon, to whom Lincoln became a mentor.

Lincoln's ambitions were not fulfilled by a successful law practice. He wanted to run for Congress from this safe Whig district, but the concentration of Whig hopefuls in Springfield meant that he had to wait his turn under an informal one-term rotation system. When his turn came in 1846, Lincoln won handily over Democratic candidate Peter Cartwright, a well-known Methodist clergyman who tried to make an issue of Lincoln's nonmembership in a church (Mary later joined Springfield's First Presbyterian Church, which Abraham also occasionally attended).

Lincoln's congressional term (1847–49) was dominated by controversies over the Mexican War. He took the standard Whig position that the war had been provoked by Democratic President James K. Polk. On December 22, 1847, Lincoln introduced "spot resolutions" calling for information on the exact "spot of soil" on which Mexicans shed American blood to start the war, implying that this spot was actually Mexican soil. Lincoln also voted several times for the Wilmot Proviso declaring that slavery should be prohibited in any territory acquired from Mexico. On these issues Lincoln sided with the majority in the Whig House of Representatives. In addition, Lincoln introduced a bill (which was buried in committee) for compensated abolition of slavery in the District of Columbia if approved by a majority of the District's voters.

Lincoln's opposition to the Mexican War was not popular in Illinois. "Spotty Lincoln," jibed Democratic newspapers, had committed political suicide. "What an epitaph: 'Died of Spotted Fever'."[11]When Lincoln campaigned in 1848 for the Whig presidential nominee Zachary Taylor, the "Spotty Lincoln" label came back to haunt him. The Whig candidate for Congress who succeeded Lincoln under the rotation system, his former law partner Stephen T. Logan, went down to defeat—perhaps because of voter backlash against the party's antiwar stance. Taylor nevertheless won the presidency, but Lincoln did not get the patronage appointment he expected as commissioner of the General Land Office. Instead, he was offered the governorship of Oregon Territory, a post he turned down.

Lincoln returned to Springfield discouraged with politics and devoted himself to practicing law. During the

1850s he became one of the leading lawyers in the state. His annual income reached $5,000. The burst of railroad construction during the decade generated a large caseload, and at various times he represented railroads. In two of his most important cases he won exemption of the Illinois Central from county taxation and successfully defended the Rock Island Railroad from a shipping company whose steamboat had hit the Rock Island's bridge over the Mississippi River (the first such bridge ever built). Yet it would be wrong to describe Lincoln as a "corporation lawyer" in the modern sense of that term. He appeared in court against corporations about as often as for them. In one important case he represented a small firm in a patent infringement suit brought against it by the McCormick Reaper Company. Lincoln continued to ride the circuit each spring and fall; the great majority of cases handled by Lincoln and Herndon (some two hundred each year) concerned local matters of debt, ejectment, slander and libel, foreclosure, divorce, and the like.

A seismic political upheaval occurred in 1854 that propelled Lincoln back into politics. The Kansas-Nebraska Act, rammed through Congress under the leadership of Illinois senator Stephen A. Douglas (an old acquaintance of Lincoln and once a rival for Mary Todd's affections), revoked the ban on slavery in the Louisiana Purchase territory north of 36° 30′. This repeal of a crucial part of the Missouri Compromise of 1820 opened Kansas Territory to slavery. It polarized the free and slave states more sharply than anything else had done. It incited several years of civil war between proslavery and antislavery forces in Kansas, which became a prelude to the national Civil War that erupted seven years later. It also gave birth to the Republican party, whose principal plank was exclusion of slavery from the territories.

Lincoln had said little in public about slavery before this moment, but during the next six years he delivered an estimated 175 speeches whose "central message" was the necessity to exclude slavery from the territories as a first step toward its ultimate extinction everywhere.[12] That had been the purpose of the Founding Fathers, Lincoln believed, when they adopted the Declaration of Independence and enacted the Northwest Ordinance of 1787 barring slavery from most of the existing territories. That was why they did not mention the words "slave" or "slavery" in the Constitution, but instead used the euphemism of "persons held to labor." "Thus, the thing is hid away, in the constitution," said Lincoln in 1854, "just as an afflicted man hides away a wen or cancer."[13] By opening all of the Louisiana Purchase territory to slavery, the Kansas-Nebraska Act had reversed the course of the Founding Fathers. That was why Lincoln was "aroused" by this law, he later recalled, "as he had never been before."[14]

Lincoln ran for the state legislature and took the stump for other "anti-Nebraska" Whigs. He offered the fullest exposition of his philosophy in a speech at Peoria on October 16, 1854. Slavery was a "monstrous injustice," he said, that "deprives our republican example of its just influence in the world—enables the enemies of free institutions, with plausibility, to taunt us as hypocrites." With the Kansas-Nebraska Act "our republican robe is soiled, and trailed in the dust. Let us repurify it.... Let us re-adopt the Declaration of Independence, and with it, the practices, and policy, which harmonize with it.... If we do this, we shall not only have saved the Union; but we shall have saved it, as to make, and keep it, forever worthy of the saving."[15] These sentiments were Lincoln's lodestar for the rest of his life.

That same year a coalition of anti-Nebraska Whigs and Democrats, including Lincoln, appeared to have gained control of the legislature. Their first task in February 1855 was to elect a U.S. senator. Because the Illinois constitution prohibited the election of a sitting member of the legislature to the Senate, Lincoln resigned his seat to become a candidate. Through six ballots he led other candidates but fell short of a majority. To prevent the election of a regular Democrat, Lincoln threw his support to Lyman Trumbull, an anti-Nebraska Democrat (soon to become a Republican), who was elected on the tenth ballot.

Deeply disappointed, Lincoln picked up his law practice again. In 1856 he helped found the Republican party in Illinois. With his speech at the new party's state convention in Bloomington on May 29 (the famous "lost speech"—so called because newspaper reporters were supposedly so entranced by its eloquence that they neglected to take it down), Lincoln emerged as the state's Republican leader. At the party's national convention he received 110 votes in a losing bid for the vice presidential nomination. Lincoln campaigned for the Republican ticket headed by John C. Frémont, giving more than fifty speeches in all parts of Illinois. While Frémont won a plurality of the Northern popular vote in the three-party contest, he lost Illinois and the other crucial lower North states of Pennsylvania and Indiana, which the Democratic candidate, James Buchanan, added to the solid South to win the presidency.

By the time Senator Douglas came up for reelection in 1858, he had broken with the Buchanan administration over the Lecompton constitution in Kansas. That constitution allegedly presented Kansas voters with a choice between admission of Kansas as a state "with slavery" or "with no slavery." But the "no slavery" charter would merely prevent the future importation of slaves into the state while protecting the slave status of those already there. Douglas denounced it as a fraud on his cherished doctrine of "popular sovereignty"—letting the voters decide whether or not to have slavery. Some Republicans in the Northeast wanted the Illinois party to support Douglas for reelection in order to widen the Democratic split.

But Illinois Republicans would have none of it. They nominated Lincoln for the Senate (an almost unprecedented procedure in that time, when state legislatures elected U.S. senators). Lincoln set the theme for his campaign with the famous "House Divided" speech at Springfield on June 16, 1858. "'A house divided against itself cannot stand,'" said Lincoln, quoting the words of Jesus recorded in the Gospel of Mark. "I believe this government cannot endure, permanently half *slave* and half *free*. . . . It will become *all* one thing, or *all* the other." The Dred Scott decision by the Supreme Court in 1857 had legalized slavery in every territory on the principle that the U.S. Constitution protected such property—a principle that Lincoln feared would legalize slavery in every state as well as territory if the Southern-dominated Supreme Court had its way. But when Republicans gained national power and had a chance to reconstitute the Court, they proposed to ban slavery from the territories, thus stifling its growth and hastening its "ultimate extinction."[16]

In the campaign, Lincoln challenged Douglas to a series of debates. Douglas accepted, and the two met in seven three-hour debates in every part of the state. Why could the country not continue to exist half slave and half free as it had for seventy years? asked Douglas. Lincoln's talk about the "ultimate extinction" of slavery would drive the South into secession. Douglas also upbraided Lincoln for his alleged belief in "negro equality." Sensing a winning issue in Illinois, where racist sentiments were strong, Douglas shouted questions to the crowd: "Are you in favor of conferring upon the negro the rights and privileges of citizenship?" Back came the response, "No, No!" "Do you desire to turn this beautiful state into a free negro colony ('no, no') in order that when Missouri abolishes slavery she can send one hundred thousand emancipated slaves into Illinois, to become citizens and voters on an equality with yourselves? ('Never,' 'no')....If you desire them to vote on an equality with yourselves...then support Mr. Lincoln and the Black Republican party, who are in favor of the citizenship of the negro. ('Never, never.')"[17]

Douglas's demagoguery put Lincoln on the defensive. A "Black Republican" would have no chance of election in Illinois. Lincoln denied Douglas's accusations. He assured his listeners that "I am not, nor ever have been, in favor of bringing about in any way the social and political equality of the white and black races (applause)."[18] On other occasions, however, Lincoln pleaded: "Let us discard all this quibbling about this man and the other man, this race and...the other race being inferior...and unite as one people throughout this land, until we shall once more stand up declaring that all men are created equal." Whether or not the black man was equal to whites in all respects, "in the right to eat the bread, without leave of anybody else, which his own hand earns, he is my equal and the equal of Judge Douglas, and the equal of every living man."[19] The real question was the morality of bondage. "That is the issue that will continue in this country when these poor tongues of Judge Douglas and myself shall be silent. It is the eternal struggle between these two principles—right and wrong—throughout the world." The problem with Douglas was that he "looks to no end of the institution of slavery," while the Republicans "will, if possible, place it where the public mind shall rest in the belief that it is in the course of ultimate extinction, in God's good time."[20]

The popular vote for Republican and Democratic legislators was virtually even in 1858, but because apportionment favored the Democrats, they won a majority of seats and reelected Douglas. Lincoln once again swallowed his disappointment and continued to speak for Republican candidates in the off-year elections of several midwestern states in 1859.

In retrospect Lincoln was the real winner of the Lincoln-Douglas debates. A question he posed to Douglas at Freeport forced his adversary to enunciate in the "Freeport Doctrine" that settlers could keep slavery out of a territory despite the Dred Scott decision legalizing it, by refusing to enact and enforce a local slave code. The Freeport Doctrine further alienated Douglas from Southern Democrats and kindled their demand for a federal slave code for the territories. This issue split the Democratic party in 1860, virtually assuring the election of a Republican president. The national visibility the debates achieved caused Lincoln's name to be increasingly mentioned as the possible Republican nominee.

While deprecating his qualifications for the presidency, Lincoln admitted privately that "the taste *is* in my mouth a little."[21] Lincoln's prospects were enhanced by the favorable impact of his speech at Cooper Union in New York City on February 27, 1860. The audience included the most influential Republicans in the media capital of the United States. On the basis of thorough research, Lincoln explicated the parallels between the Republican position on slavery and that of the Founding Fathers: they too had believed that Congress could exclude slavery from the territories and looked forward to its ultimate disappearance. Lincoln's speech dazzled this important audience, many of whom had not expected much from the gangly midwesterner in ill-fitting clothes. "He held the vast meeting spellbound," wrote one listener. "I think I never saw an audience more carried away by an orator."[22] Lincoln's concluding sentence brought all to their feet with an ovation that went on and on: "LET US HAVE FAITH THAT RIGHT MAKES MIGHT, AND IN THAT FAITH, LET US, TO THE END, DARE TO DO OUR DUTY AS WE UNDERSTAND IT."[23]

Lincoln's success at Cooper Union brought him numerous invitations to speak in New England on his way to visit his oldest son Robert, who had enrolled at Phillips Exeter Academy for a year of preparatory work before entering Harvard. Lincoln used these occasions to focus on what has been called the "free labor ideology," which was at the core of the Republican value system. All work in a free society was honorable. Slavery degraded manual labor by equating it with bondage. Free men who practiced the virtues of industry, thrift, self-discipline, and sobriety could climb the ladder of success. "I am not ashamed to confess," Lincoln said in New Haven, "that twenty-five years ago I was a hired laborer, mauling rails, at work on a flat-boat—just what might happen to any poor man's son." But in the free states an ambitious man "can better his condition" because "there is no such thing as a freeman being fatally fixed for life, in the condition of a hired laborer." The lack of hope, energy, and progress in the slave states, where most laborers *were* "fatally fixed" in the condition of bondage, had made the United States a house divided. Republicans wanted to keep slavery out of the territories so that white farmers and workers could move there to better their condition without being "degraded...by forced rivalry with negro slaves." Moreover, said Lincoln, "I want every man to have the chance—and I believe a black man is entitled to it—in which he *can* better his condition."[24] The symbolism of Lincoln, the "poor man's son," visiting his own son at New England's most elite school was not lost on his audiences.

Lincoln returned from his triumphant Eastern tour to find Illinois friends mounting a concerted effort for his nomination as president. As the May 16 opening date approached for the Republican National Convention in Chicago (a fortunate location for Lincoln's cause), circumstances converted him from a favorite son to a serious contender. The leading candidate was Senator William H. Seward of New York. Seward's long and prominent public career was a source of both strength and weakness, for he could claim leadership experience but had made powerful enemies in the course of gaining that experience. His chief liability was a reputation as an antislavery radical who could not carry the crucial lower-North states of Illinois, Indiana, and Pennsylvania that the Republicans had lost in 1856. Although Seward's current position was actually more conservative in some respects than Lincoln's, he suffered from the image created by his famous Higher Law and Irrepressible Conflict speeches in 1850 and 1858. There is a higher law than the Constitution, Seward had said in a speech opposing the Compromise of 1850, the law of God in which all people are free and equal. In 1858 Seward had described an irrepressible conflict between slavery and freedom in which freedom was sure to triumph. This argument was little different from Lincoln's House Divided speech, but Seward's prominence made him seem a more dangerous radical than Lincoln. The latter's campaign managers worked feverishly to persuade delegates to the Republican convention that their man was more electable than Seward and to line up second-choice commitments to Lincoln from several states. They also skillfully exploited Lincoln's "rail-splitter" image to illustrate the party's free-labor theme. The strategy worked. Seward led on the first ballot; Lincoln almost caught up on the second and won on the third.

The ensuing four-party campaign was the most fateful in American history. The Democrats split into Northern and Southern parties, while a remnant of Whigs, mostly from the border states, formed the Constitutional Union party. Lincoln carried every free state except New Jersey, whose electoral votes he divided with Douglas, and thereby won the election despite garnering slighly less than 40 percent of the popular votes—no popular votes were cast in ten Southern states. Seven of those states enacted ordinances of secession before Lincoln's inauguration.

Between the election and his inauguration, Lincoln remained in Springfield, putting together an administration. He made no public statements despite panicky advice that he should say something to reassure the South. He was already on record many times saying that he had no constitutional power and no intention to interfere with slavery in the states where it existed. "I have said this so often already," he wrote, "that a repetition of it is but mockery, bearing an appearance of weakness." Lincoln would have been willing to repeat these statements "if there were no danger of encouraging bold bad men...who are eager for something new upon which to base new misrepresentations—men who would like to frighten me, or, at least, to fix upon me the character of timidity and cowardice. They would seize upon almost any letter I could write, as being an '*awful coming down.*'"[25]

Lincoln gave private assurances to Southern moderates and Unionists that he would go no farther against slavery than the Republican platform's pledge to keep it out of the territories. To Alexander Stephens of Georgia, who opposed secession until his state went out, Lincoln wrote in December that the slave states had nothing to fear from him, but added: "I suppose, however, this does not meet the case. You think slavery is *right* and ought to be extended; while we think it is *wrong* and ought to be restricted. That I suppose is the rub."[26]

It was indeed the rub. Southerners had read Lincoln's House Divided speech, in which he had said that restricting slavery's expansion was a first step toward "ultimate extinction." Whether ultimate or imminent, the dreaded demise of slavery portended by the South's loss of the national administration to an antislavery party was the reason to secede. For most secessionists there was no turning back.

Nevertheless, a host of compromise proposals emerged during the 1860–61 session of Congress. The most important were embodied in constitutional amendments sponsored by Senator John J. Crittenden of Kentucky. The centerpiece of the Crittenden Compromise was a proposal to allow slavery south of 36° 30′ in all territories "now held, *or hereafter acquired*" (italics added). Such a compromise would not only negate the chief plank of the Republican platform but would also step up the drive to acquire Cuba and other tropical territories suitable for slavery. Seward (whom Lincoln intended to appoint as secretary of state) and some other Republicans seemed prepared to tilt toward compromise. But from Springfield came admonitions to stand firm. "Entertain no proposition for a compromise in regard to the *extension* of slavery," Lincoln wrote to Seward and to other key Republican leaders. "The instant you do, they have us under again; all our labor is lost, and sooner or later must be done over.... Filibustering for all South of us, and making slave states of it, would follow." The Republicans had won the election "on principles fairly stated to the people.... If we surrender, it is the end of us, and of the government. They will repeat the experiment on us *ad libitum*. A year will not pass, till we shall have to take Cuba as a condition upon which they will stay in the Union."[27]

The Crittenden Compromise went down in defeat, but there is no reason to believe that the seven seceded states would have returned even if it had passed. These states had seized all federal property within their borders except Fort Pickens on an island off Pensacola and Fort Sumter in Charleston harbor, plus two forts on the Florida Keys. A month before Congress adjourned (and before Lincoln was inaugurated), delegates from the seven seceded states met at Montgomery, Alabama, and formed the Confederate States of America. As he departed from Springfield for Washington on February 11, "with a task before me greater than rested upon Washington," Lincoln faced the stark reality of a divided nation.[28]

Lincoln's inaugural address offered both a sword and an olive branch to the South. The sword was an unconditional affirmation of the illegality of secession and of his intention to execute the laws in all states, to "hold, occupy and possess" federal property, and to "collect the [customs] duties and imposts." The olive branch was a reiteration of Lincoln's pledge not "to interfere with slavery where it exists" and to enforce the constitutional provision for the return of fugitive slaves. Wherever "in any interior locality" hostility to the federal government was "so great and so universal, as to prevent competent resident citizens from holding the Federal offices," Lincoln would suspend federal operations "for the time." In an eloquent peroration (rewritten from phrases suggested by Seward), Lincoln appealed to Southerners to reconsider their rash actions. "In *your* hands, my dissatisfied fellow countrymen, and not in *mine*, is the momentous issue of civil war....We are not enemies, but friends. We must not be enemies. Though passion may have strained, it must not break our bonds of affection. The mystic chords of memory, stretching from every battlefield, and patriot grave, to every living heart and hearthstone, all over this broad land, will yet swell the chorus of the Union, when again touched, as surely they will be, by the better angels of our nature."[29]

Lincoln hoped that his inaugural address would buy time for tempers to cool off in the South and enable the seven states to "reconstruct" themselves back into the Union. This hope was founded on an erroneous but widely shared assumption in the North that a silent majority of Southerners were really Unionists who had been swept along by the passions of the moment. But time was running out. The day after his inauguration, Lincoln learned that Major Robert Anderson, commander of the besieged federal garrison at Fort Sumter in Charleston harbor, had supplies enough only to last a few more weeks.

Fort Sumter was the flash point of tension, and Charleston was proud of its reputation as the cradle of secession. Insisting that a sovereign nation could not tolerate a foreign port in one of its harbors, Confederate leaders demanded the transfer of Fort Sumter to the Confederacy. For a month Lincoln endured sleepless nights and conflicting advice on what to do. To give it up would constitute de facto if not de jure recognition of the Confederacy. It would undoubtedly cause foreign nations to extend diplomatic recognition to the Confederacy as an independent nation. On the other hand, withdrawing from Sumter would preserve the peace and perhaps keep other slave states from seceding. On March 15 a majority of the cabinet, with Seward as the strongest voice, counseled Lincoln to yield Fort Sumter. Lincoln explored the possibility of pulling out in return for an assurance from Virginia that it would remain in the Union. "A State for a fort is no bad business," Lincoln supposedly said.[30] Playing an independent role as the putative "premier" of the administration, Seward informed Confederate commissioners that Lincoln would withdraw the garrison. By the end of March, however, the president had made the opposite decision. He let Seward know in no uncertain terms that he would be premier of his own administration.

A majority of the cabinet now supported Lincoln's decision to resupply Fort Sumter (as well as the less controversial Fort Pickens). The problem was how to do it. Sending reinforcements prepared to shoot their way into Charleston Bay would surely provoke a war that Lincoln would be blamed for starting. But Lincoln hit upon an ingenious solution. Instead of sending troops, he would send only provisions—"food for hungry men"—and he would notify Southern authorities in advance of his peaceful intentions. On April 6 Lincoln sent a message to the governor of South Carolina: "An attempt will be made to supply Fort-Sumpter [sic] with provisions only; and that, if such attempt be not resisted, no effort to throw in men, arms, or ammunition, will be made, without further notice, or in case of an attack upon the Fort."[31]

With this message Lincoln in effect flipped a coin and told Confederate president Jefferson Davis, "Heads I win; tails you lose." If the Confederates allowed the supplies to pass, the American flag would continue to fly over Fort Sumter as a symbol of sovereignty. If the Confederates attacked the supply ships or the fort with their artillery that ringed the bay, they would suffer the onus of starting a war and would unite a divided North. Davis did not hesitate; he ordered the Confederate guns to fire on Sumter. They did so on April 12. And the war came.

On April 15 Lincoln called up 75,000 militia to quell the rebellion, prompting four more states to secede. On April 19 Lincoln proclaimed a naval blockade of the Confederate coastline. From there the war escalated step by step on a scale of violence and destruction never dreamed of by those who fired the guns at Sumter. By the end of the war in April 1865, 2.2 million men had fought in Union armies and navies, and about 850,000 had fought for the Confederacy. More than 620,000 of these soldiers and sailors died in the struggle.

The Civil War took on such large and destructive proportions because it was fought over a nonnegotiable central issue. No compromise between a sovereign *United* States and a separately sovereign *Confederate* States was possible. "The central idea pervading this struggle," said

Lincoln in 1861, "is the necessity that is upon us, of proving that popular government is not an absurdity. We must settle this question now, whether in a free government the minority have the right to break up the government whenever they choose."[32] Secession "is the essence of anarchy," said Lincoln on another occasion, for if one state may secede at will, so may any other until there is no government and no nation. In his address at the dedication of the soldiers' cemetery at Gettysburg in November 1863, Lincoln offered his most eloquent statement of the war's purpose: it tested whether the nation conceived in 1776 "might live" or would "perish from the earth." This issue "is distinct, simple, and inflexible," said Lincoln a year later. It is an issue which can only be tried by war, and decided by victory."[33]

Because "all else chiefly depends" on "the progress of our arms," as Lincoln said in 1865, he devoted more attention to his duties as commander in chief than to any other function of the presidency. He spent a great deal of time in the War Department telegraph office reading reports from his generals and sending instructions to them. He borrowed books on military history and strategy from the Library of Congress and other sources, and burned the midnight oil mastering them. Eleven times he visited troops at the front in Virginia or Maryland, spending a total of forty-two days with the army. The greatest frustrations he experienced were the failures of several Union generals to act with the vigor and aggressiveness he expected of them. Perhaps one of the greatest satisfactions he experienced was the ultimate success of other commanders who had risen to the top in large part because Lincoln appreciated their vigor and aggressiveness.

In 1861 Union armies achieved limited but important successes by gaining control of Maryland, Missouri, part of Kentucky, and also much of western Virginia, which paved the way for the later admission of West Virginia as a new state. Meanwhile, Union naval forces gained lodgments along the South Atlantic coast. But in the year's biggest battle, at Bull Run (Manassas) on July 21, the Union suffered a dispiriting defeat. Lincoln then appointed thirty-four-year-old George B. McClellan commander of the Army of the Potomac and, from November 1, general in chief of all Union armies. McClellan's minor victories in western Virginia had given him a newspaper reputation as the "Young Napoleon" who would make short work of the rebellion. He proved to be a superb organizer and trainer of soldiers but a defensive-minded and cautious perfectionist in action. Repeatedly he exaggerated enemy strength as an excuse for postponing offensive operations.

Lincoln grew impatient with McClellan's inaction during the eight months after he took command of the Army of the Potomac. Republicans in Congress grew suspicious that McClellan, a Democrat, did not really want to strike the "rebels" a hard blow. When McClellan finally began a glacial advance toward Richmond up the Virginia peninsula in the spring of 1862, Lincoln admonished him on April 9: "Once more let me tell you, it is indispensable to *you* that you strike a blow.... I have never written you, or spoken to you, in greater kindness of feeling than now, nor with a fuller purpose to sustain you.... *But you must act*."[34]

Lincoln already had his eye on a commander who had proved that he could act. His name was Ulysses S. Grant. He had captured Forts Henry and Donelson on the Tennessee and Cumberland rivers in February and then had beaten back a Confederate counteroffensive in the bloody battle of Shiloh on April 6–7. Other Union forces in the West also scored important victories in the spring of 1862, capturing New Orleans and Memphis, and gaining control of most of the Mississippi River. In Virginia McClellan finally advanced to within six miles of Richmond by the end of May. The Confederacy seemed doomed.

Then the Union war machine went into reverse. By September 1862 Confederate counteroffensives in Virginia, Tennessee, and Kentucky took Southern armies across the Potomac River into Maryland and almost north to the Ohio River. This reversal of momentum stunned

Northerners and caused home-front morale to plummet, but Lincoln did not falter. He issued a new call for volunteers and declared that "I expect to maintain this contest until successful, or till I die, or am conquered, or my term expires, or Congress or the country forsakes me."[35]

The Confederate tide ebbed as limited Union victories at Antietam on September 17 and Perryville on October 8 turned back the Confederate invasions of Maryland and Kentucky. But the failure of Union commanders to follow up these victories caused Lincoln's frustration to boil over. He could not "understand why we cannot march as the enemy marches, live as he lives, fight as he fights."[36] On October 24 he replaced sluggish General Don Carlos Buell with General William S. Rosecrans as commander of the Army of the Ohio (renamed the Army of the Cumberland). Two weeks later he removed McClellan from command of the Army of the Potomac (he had already been demoted from general in chief). Lincoln told one of McClellan's supporters that he could no longer "bore with an auger too dull to take hold."[37]

But Lincoln did not have any better luck with the next two commanders of the Army of the Potomac. General Ambrose Burnside lost the disastrous battle of Fredericksburg on December 13, 1862, and his successor General Joseph Hooker fumbled several opportunities and lost the battle of Chancellorsville on May 1–5,

1863. Lincoln finally found a general who remained in command of that army for the rest of the war, George G. Meade, whose skillful defensive tactics won the crucial battle of Gettysburg on July 1–3, 1863. Meade gravely disappointed Lincoln, however, by failing to follow up that victory with a vigorous effort to trap and destroy General Robert E. Lee's Army of Northern Virginia before it could retreat across the Potomac River swollen by recent heavy rains. "My dear general, I do not believe you appreciate the magnitude of the misfortune involved in Lee's escape," Lincoln wrote to Meade on July 14. "He was within your easy grasp, and to have closed upon him would, in connection with our other late successes [the capture of Confederate fortifications on the Mississippi River at Vicksburg and Port Hudson, along with their 36,000 defenders] have ended the war. As it is, the war will be prolonged indefinitely.... Your golden opportunity is gone, and I am distressed immeasurably because of it."[38]

Upon reflection, Lincoln filed this letter away unsent. But it expressed his sentiments, sharpened by contrast with his attitude toward Grant, who had captured Vicksburg on July 4, 1863. Grant's star had alternately brightened and dimmed and brightened again since the spring of 1862. Unfounded rumors of his drunkenness before the battle of Shiloh and the appearance of aimless floundering in the early stages of the Vicksburg campaign had generated much criticism. Twice Lincoln came under great pressure to remove Grant from command. One of the president's greatest contributions to ultimate Union victory however, was his decision to defend Grant and to stick with him. One of Grant's supporters, Representative Elihu B. Washburne of Illinois, told the general that "when the torrent of obloquy and detraction was rolling over you, and your friends, after the battle of Shiloh, Mr. Lincoln stood like a wall of fire between you and it, uninfluenced by the threats of Congressmen and the demands of insolent cowardice."[39] Lincoln himself said that "I have had stronger influence brought against Grant, praying for his removal, since the battle of Pittsburg Landing [Shiloh], than for any other object, coming too from good men. . . . If I had done as my Washington friends, who fight battles with their tongues instead of swords far from the enemy, demanded of me, Grant, who has proved himself so great a military captain, would never have been heard of again."[40]

Grant followed up his victory at Vicksburg by driving the Confederates away from Chattanooga and into the mountains of northern Georgia. Congress then created the rank of lieutenant general (last held by George Washington). Lincoln promoted Grant to this rank in March 1864 and made him general in chief of all Union armies. For the first time Lincoln had a commanding general in whom he had full confidence, one who could take from his shoulders some of the burden of constant military oversight. "You are vigilant and self-reliant," Lincoln told Grant on the eve of the spring military campaigns in 1864, "and pleased with this, I wish not to obtrude any constraints or restraints upon you."[41]

Lincoln wrote these words because he knew that he and Grant saw eye to eye on military strategy. In this war, the Confederates had the advantage of fighting on the strategic defensive with interior lines that enabled them to shift reinforcements from inactive to active fronts unless the Union employed its superior numbers to attack on several fronts at once. Lincoln grasped this point better than many of his generals. As early as January 13, 1862, he wrote to Generals Henry W. Halleck and Don Carlos Buell, whose respective armies he wanted to advance simultaneously against Confederate positions in Kentucky: "I state my general idea of this war to be that we have *greater* numbers, and the enemy has the *greater* facility of concentrating forces upon points of collision; that we must fail, unless we can find some way of making *our* advantage an overmatch for *his*; and that this can only be done by menacing him with superior forces at *different* points, at the *same* time."[42] Grant agreed. He ordered five separate Union armies across a thousand miles of battle-front to advance simultaneously against as many smaller

Confederate armies in the spring of 1864 to prevent any one of them from reinforcing another. Lincoln was impressed. He told his private secretary John Hay that Grant's plans reminded him of his own "suggestion so constantly made and as constantly neglected, to Buell & Halleck et al to move at once upon the enemy's whole line so as to bring into action our great superiority in numbers."[43] In the end, this strategy won the war.

An issue related to military events also absorbed much of Lincoln's time: internal security. Confederate sympathizers in the border states and antiwar activists in the North (the "Copperheads") constituted a "fire in the rear" that Lincoln said he feared "more than our military chances."[44] When pro-Confederate elements in Maryland burned bridges and tore down telegraph wires in the early weeks of the war, isolating Washington from the North, Lincoln suspended the writ of habeas corpus so these activists could be arrested and imprisoned. The president subsequently expanded the areas where the writ was suspended, and by the time the war was over at least fifteen thousand people had been arrested and placed in "preventive detention," mainly in the border slave states. (Most were released if they took an oath of allegiance to the United States.)

Lincoln's initial suspension of the writ led to a confrontation with Chief Justice Roger Taney. In his capacity as a circuit court judge in Maryland, Taney ruled in May 1861 that the president could not suspend the writ without congressional authorization.[45] The U.S. Constitution specifies that "The Privilege of the Writ of Habeas Corpus shall not be suspended, unless when in Cases of Rebellion or Invasion the public Safety may require it." At issue was not whether the writ could be suspended, but *who* could suspend it. Because this provision is in Article I of the Constitution, which deals with the powers of Congress, Taney stated that only Congress had the power to authorize suspension. Lincoln disagreed, insisting that suspension was an emergency wartime action that fell within his powers as commander in chief. "As commander-in-chief of the army and navy, in time of war," he wrote, "I suppose I have a right to take any measure which may best subdue the enemy."[46]

In 1862 Lincoln also authorized the creation of military tribunals to try civilians engaged in efforts to undermine the war effort. (After the war, the Supreme Court declared such trials unconstitutional in areas where the civil courts had been open.) The most famous such trial occurred in May 1863, when a military tribunal convicted the prominent Copperhead Clement L. Vallandigham of Ohio for speaking against the war, the draft, and emancipation. Some of these arrests and trials, including the Vallandigham case, came dangerously close to infringing

First Amendment rights. Lincoln was embarrassed by Vallandigham's arrest, which he did not learn about until after it took place. Nevertheless, he justified the detention of those who sabotaged the struggle for national survival. He made his case in forceful prose that everyone could understand. "Under cover of 'Liberty of speech,' 'Liberty of the press' and '*Habeas Corpus*,'" he wrote in a public letter published in numerous newspapers, that the rebels "hoped to keep on foot amongst us a most efficient corps of spies, informers, suppliers, and aiders and abettors of their cause." If anything, he believed he had arrested too few rather than too many. "Must I shoot a simple-minded soldier boy who deserts, while I must not touch a hair of a wily agitator who induces him to desert? . . . I think that in such a case, to silence the agitator, and save the boy, is not only constitutional, but, withal, a great mercy."[47] Historians disagree about Lincoln's record on civil liberties, but one thing can be said with certainty: compared with the enforcement of espionage and sedition laws in World War I and the internment of Japanese-Americans in World War II, the curtailment of civil liberties during the far greater internal crisis of the Civil War seems to have been quite mild.

Another matter bound up with Lincoln's powers as commander in chief, but involving many other considerations as well, was slavery. Lincoln's decision in 1862 to issue an emancipation proclamation freed himself as much as it freed the slaves—freed him from the agonizing contradiction between his antislavery convictions and his constitutional obligations. Lincoln had said many times that he considered slavery "a social, moral, and political wrong.... If slavery is not wrong, nothing is wrong." Yet, he added, "I have never understood that the Presidency conferred upon me an unrestricted right to act officially on this judgment and feeling."[48] The Constitution he had sworn to preserve, protect, and defend sanctioned slavery in states that wanted it. Moreover, Lincoln conceived his primary duty to be the preservation of the Union. In

1861 he believed that preserving it meant maintaining the support of Democrats and border-state Unionists for the war effort. They would be alienated by any move toward emancipation. That is why he revoked General John C. Frémont's military order freeing the slaves of Confederate sympathizers in Missouri. If he had let Frémont's order stand, Lincoln explained to a critic, it would have driven Kentucky into the arms of the Confederacy. "To lose Kentucky is nearly the same as to lose the whole game. Kentucky gone, we can not hold Missouri, nor, as I think, Maryland. These all against us, and the job on our hands is too large for us. We would as well consent to separation at once, including the surrender of this capitol."[49]

For the next year Lincoln adhered publicly to this position despite growing pressure from his own party to move against slavery. To a powerful emancipation editorial by Horace Greeley in the *New York Tribune*, Lincoln replied on August 22, 1862, with a letter published in many newspapers: "My paramount object in this struggle *is* to save the Union, and is *not* either to save or to destroy slavery. If I could save the Union without freeing *any* slave I would do it; and if I could save it by freeing *all* the slaves I would do it; and if I could save it by freeing some and leaving others alone I would also do that." Lincoln concluded with an assertion that this was his "view of *official* duty; and I intend no modification of my oft-expressed *personal* wish that all men every where could be free."[50]

When he wrote this letter, Lincoln had already drafted an emancipation proclamation but was awaiting a Union military victory to give it impetus and credibility. His letter to Greeley was designed to prepare the public, especially conservatives and those Kentuckians he had worried about the previous year, for the announcement by making it clear that freeing *some* of the slaves might be necessary to achieve his, and their, main goal of preserving the Union.

Earlier in 1862 Lincoln had tried to persuade border-state Unionists to accept an offer of federal compensation for voluntary emancipation in their states. They refused, while Union military fortunes took a turn for the worse in the summer of 1862. By then Lincoln agreed with the Radical Republican argument that a proclamation of emancipation would strike a blow against the Confederate economy and war effort that would more than counterbalance the damage it might do by alienating Democrats and border-state Unionists. Slaves constituted the principal labor force of the Confederacy. Escaped slaves (labeled "contrabands") had been entering Union lines since the beginning of the war; an official proclamation of freedom would accelerate that process. In his capacity as commander in chief, Lincoln believed that he had the constitutional power to seize enemy property (slaves) being used to wage war against the United States. "Decisive and extreme measure must be adopted," Lincoln told members of the cabinet in July 1862, according to Secretary of the Navy Gideon Welles. Emancipation was "a military necessity, absolutely necessary to the preservation of the Union. We must free the slaves or be ourselves subdued. The slaves [are] undeniably an element of strength to those who have their service, and we must decide whether that element should be with us or against us.... We [want] the army to strike more vigorous blows. The administration must set the army an example and strike at the heart of the rebellion."[51]

On September 22, 1862, five days after the battle of Antietam, Lincoln issued a preliminary proclamation declaring that all slaves in any state or part of a state still in rebellion against the United States on January 1, 1863, "shall be then, thenceforward, and forever free."[52] New Year's Day came, and Lincoln issued the Emancipation Proclamation, which exempted Tennessee and parts of Louisiana and Virginia (as well as the slave states that had remained in the Union), because they were occupied by Union forces or deemed loyal to the Union and therefore not subject to the war powers under which Lincoln acted.

These exemptions produced cavils that the Emancipation Proclamation did not in and of itself free a single slave, and that Lincoln proclaimed slaves free where he had no power to enforce the edict and did not touch slavery where he did have the power. These claims are false in several respects. He had no power to seize slaves as enemy property from owners who were not enemies. Tens of thousands of slaves and "contrabands" lived in parts of North and South Carolina, Georgia, Florida, Mississippi, and Arkansas occupied by Union forces but to which the proclamation did apply. Many slaves in these areas celebrated January 1 as Emancipation Day. Elsewhere, the proclamation announced a purpose to free slaves when (and if) Union armies conquered the Confederacy. The proclamation made Union armies into armies of liberation. The Declaration of Independence in 1776 had not made the United States an independent nation. That was accomplished only by victory in the War of the Revolution. Freedom for slaves would likewise be accomplished only by victory in the War for the Union.

As a corollary of the Emancipation Proclamation, the Lincoln administration began recruiting black soldiers and sailors—mostly freed slaves—almost 200,000 in all by the end of the war. In August 1863 Lincoln stated in a widely published letter that "the emancipation policy, and the use of colored troops, constitute the heaviest blow yet dealt to the rebellion." Referring to critics of emancipation and opponents of the war, Lincoln said pointedly that when the war was won, "there will be some black men who can remember that, with silent tongue, and clenched teeth, and steady eye, and well-poised bayonet, they have helped mankind on to this great consummation; while, I fear, there will be some white ones, unable to forget that, with malignant heart, and deceitful speech, they have strove to hinder it."[53]

Lincoln defended the constitutionality of the Emancipation Proclamation on the same grounds as he justified his suspension of habeas corpus: as commander in chief "I have a right to take any measure which may best subdue the enemy." He also offered an analogy that was clear and powerful during this war in which so many wounded soldiers experienced amputation of an arm or leg in order to save their lives. "By general law life *and* limb must be protected," said Lincoln, "yet often a limb must be amputated to save a life; but a life is never wisely given to save a limb. I felt that measures, otherwise unconstitutional, might become lawful, by becoming indispensable to preservation of the constitution, through preservation of the nation. . . . In our case, the moment came when I felt that slavery must die that the nation might live!"[54]

As a war measure, the Emancipation Proclamation would cease to have any effect when the war was over. While many slaves would have gained freedom, the institution of slavery would still exist. Thus Lincoln and his party pledged to adopt a constitutional amendment to abolish slavery. Even before that Thirteenth Amendment became part of the Constitution after the war was over, antislavery Unionists gained control of the state governments of Maryland and Missouri, and abolished slavery in those states. The wartime reconstruction governments in the Union-occupied parts of Louisiana, Arkansas, and Tennessee did the same. With a skillful use of patronage and arm-twisting, Lincoln nurtured these achievements.

Lincoln did not live to see the final ratification of the Thirteenth Amendment. Yet the future shape of a disenthralled United States was clear enough by November 19, 1863, for Lincoln to proclaim "a new birth of freedom" in the address he delivered at the commemoration of a cemetery at Gettysburg for Union soldiers killed in the battle there. The most famous speech in American history, it was only 272 words in length and took two minutes to deliver. This elegant prose poem is constructed of three parallel sets of three images each that are intricately interwoven: past, present, future; continent, nation, battlefield; and birth, death, rebirth. Four score and seven years in the *past* our fathers *conceived* and *brought forth* on this *continent* a *nation* that stood for something important in the world: the proposition that all men are created equal. *Now*, our generation faces a great war testing whether such a nation standing for such an ideal can survive. In dedicating the cemetery on this *battlefield*, the living must take inspiration to finish the task that those who lie buried here nobly advanced by giving the last full measure of their devotion. Life and death in this passage have a paradoxical relationship: men died that the nation might live, yet the old Union also died, and with it must die the institution of slavery. After these deaths, the nation must have a "new birth of freedom" so that government of, by, and for the people that our fathers conceived and brought forth in the past "shall not perish from the earth" but be preserved as a legacy for the *future*.

℃

Abraham Lincoln's eloquence and statesmanship were grounded in his skills as a politician. He was not only president and commander in chief but also leader of his party. Some of the party's more fractious members in the cabinet and Congress gave Lincoln almost as many problems as did fractious or incompetent generals. Four members of the original cabinet had been his rivals for the presidential nomination in 1860. Some of them as well as some congressional leaders continued to consider themselves better qualified for the presidency than Lincoln. Yet he established his mastery of both cabinet and Congress. He generally deferred to cabinet members in their areas of responsibility and delegated administrative authority to them to run their departments. Although he listened to advice, Lincoln made the most important decisions himself: on Fort Sumter, on emancipation, on appointing or removing generals, on Reconstruction. Secretary of the Treasury Salmon P. Chase, who was thinking of running for president in 1864, convinced Republican senators that Lincoln was overly influenced by Secretary of State Seward. At a low point in the Union cause after the battle of Fredericksburg in December 1862, the Senate Republican caucus pressed Lincoln to dismiss Seward. If he had "caved in" (Lincoln's words) to this demand, he would have lost control of his own administration. In an exhibition of political virtuosity, Lincoln confronted Chase and the senators in the presence of the cabinet and forced them to back down. Chase offered his resignation, which Lincoln refused to accept, thereby keeping both Seward and Chase in the cabinet and maintaining the separation of executive and congressional powers.

Another contest of power and policy between Lincoln and congressional Republicans occurred in 1864 over the issue of Reconstruction. Lincoln conceived of this process as primarily an executive responsibility, a part of his duty as commander in chief to win the war by "reconstructing" Southern states back into the Union. On December 8, 1863, he issued a "Proclamation of Amnesty and Reconstruction," offering pardons to most categories of Confederates who would take an oath of allegiance to the United States. When the number of those pardoned in any state equaled 10 percent of the number of voters in 1860, Lincoln authorized them to form a Union state government, to which he promised executive recognition. Congressional leaders, however, viewed Reconstruction as a legislative process in which Congress would mandate the conditions for restoration of states to the Union and for readmission of their representatives to Congress. The showdown in this struggle came in the summer of 1864, when Lincoln killed the Wade-Davis Reconstruction bill, which was more stringent than his own policy, by a pocket veto. The bill's co-sponsors, Representative Henry Winter Davis and Senator Benjamin Wade, thereupon issued a blistering "Manifesto" charging Lincoln with executive usurpation.

This imbroglio became entangled with Lincoln's campaign for reelection. The party's national convention had unanimously renominated him on June 7 after an initial token vote for Grant by the Missouri delegation. But beneath this surface unanimity seethed hostility to Lincoln by Republicans who opposed him on Reconstruction. The main issue in the summer of 1864, however, was not Reconstruction but the course of the war itself. Union offensives, especially in Virginia, became bogged down in a morass of carnage that made victory appear more distant than ever. War weariness and defeatism corroded the will of Northerners as they reeled from the staggering cost in lives. The influential *New York Tribune* editor Horace Greeley wrote to Lincoln on July 7: "Our bleeding, bankrupt, almost dying country longs for peace—shudders at the prospect of fresh conscriptions, of further wholesale devastations, and of new rivers of human blood."[55]

Lincoln came under enormous pressure to open peace negotiations to end the seemingly endless slaughter. In response, he authorized Greeley to meet with Confederate agents in Canada, and also sanctioned an informal meeting in Richmond between two Northern citizens and Confederate president Jefferson Davis. Lincoln clearly spelled out his terms for peace: "Any proposition which embraces the restoration of peace, the integrity of the whole Union, and the abandonment of slavery, and which comes by and with an authority that can control the armies now at war with the United States will be received and considered."[56]

Of course Jefferson Davis spurned these terms of reunion and abandonment of slavery. Lincoln had expected him to do so, and hoped that this rejection would convince the Northerners that peace with reunion could be achieved only by military victory. But Democrats and even some Republicans fastened on Lincoln's second condition for peace—abolition of slavery—as the sole stumbling block to negotiations, even though no evidence existed that Davis would agree to peace negotiations if that condition was dropped. Nonetheless, Lincoln was subjected to renewed pressure to drop the "abandonment of slavery" condition. He refused to do so. "No human power can subdue this rebellion without using the Emancipation lever as I have done," he declared. Lincoln pointed out that more than 100,000 black soldiers and sailors were fighting for the Union at that moment. "If they stake their lives for us they must be prompted by the strongest motive—even the promise of freedom. And the promise being made, must be kept." To jettison emancipation as a condition of peace would "ruin the Union cause itself," he continued. "All recruiting of colored men would instantly cease, and all colored men in our service would instantly desert us. And rightfully too. Why should they give their lives for us, with full notice of our purpose to betray them? . . . I should be damned in time and eternity for so doing. The world shall know that I will keep my faith to friends and enemies, come what will."[57]

When Lincoln said this, he fully expected to lose the election in November. On August 23 he wrote his famous "blind memorandum" and required cabinet members to endorse it sight unseen (evidently to prevent a leak): "This morning, as for some days past, it seems exceedingly probable that this Administration will not be re-elected. Then it will be my duty to so co-operate with the President elect, as to save the Union between the election and the inauguration; as he will have secured his election on such ground that he can not possibly save it afterwards."[58] A week later the Democrats nominated George B. McClellan for president on a platform that declared: "After four years of failure to restore the Union by the experiment of war ... [we] demand that immediate efforts be made for a cessation of hostilities, with a view to an ultimate convention of the states, or other peaceable means, to the end that, at the earliest practicable moment, peace my be restored on the basis of the Federal Union."[59]

Lincoln was quite correct to say that the election of a candidate on this platform would be interpreted as a repudiation by Northern voters of his policy of restoring the Union and abolishing slavery by winning the war. If the election had been held on the day the Democrats adopted this platform, they probably would have won. But three days later, on September 3, a telegram arrived in Washington from General William T. Sherman: "Atlanta is ours, and fairly won."[60] The impact of this news was astonishing. It turned Northern opinion about the success or failure of the war 180 degrees almost overnight. Then came additional news in September and October of spectacular military victories by General Philip Sheridan's army in the Shenandoah Valley. Lincoln's tarnished reputation as commander in chief started to regain some luster. He was triumphantly reelected in November, carrying every Union state except New Jersey, Delaware, and Kentucky.

As Sherman marched through Georgia and South Carolina, Union armies advanced on other fronts and Grant tightened the vise around Richmond. The end of the war seemed only a matter of time. In his second inaugural address, on March 4, 1865, Lincoln looked forward to a peace "with malice toward none; with charity for all." He also suggested that "this terrible war" may have been God's punishment of the whole nation, North as well as South, for the evil of slavery. "Fondly do we hope—fervently do we pray—that this mighty scourge of war may speedily pass away," said Lincoln. "Yet, if God wills that it continue, until all the wealth piled by the bond-man's two hundred and fifty years of unrequited toil shall be sunk, and until every drop of blood drawn with the lash, shall be paid by another drawn with the sword, as was said three thousand years ago, so still it must be said 'the judgments of the Lord, are true and righteous altogether.' "[61]

Lincoln happened to be visiting General Grant and the Army of the Potomac at the front when Union forces broke Confederate defenses at Petersburg and compelled General Robert E. Lee and the Army of Northern Virginia to evacuate both Petersburg and Richmond on April 2. "Thank God I have lived to see this!" Lincoln told Admiral David D. Porter, commander of the Union fleet in the James River. "It seems to me that I have been dreaming a horrid dream, and now the nightmare is gone. I want to see Richmond."[62] Escorted only by ten sailors from Porter's flagship, Lincoln and his twelve-year-old son Tad landed in Richmond on April 4 and walked the streets of the Confederate capital. The news quickly spread that the Emancipator had arrived, and thousands of freed slaves crowded to see the Moses they believed had led them to freedom. "I know that I am free," shouted one woman, "for I have seen father Abraham and felt him." To one black man who fell on his knees before him, an embarrassed Lincoln said: "Don't kneel to me. That is not right. You must kneel to God only and thank him for the liberty you will hereafter enjoy." The president was profoundly moved by these encounters. But sitting in Jefferson Davis's chair in the Confederate White House only two days after Davis had vacated it may have given him the most satisfaction.[63]

During the last winter of war, Lincoln and congressional Republicans came closer together on a postwar Reconstruction policy. After Lee's surrender at Appomattox, Lincoln spoke to a large crowd of celebrants on April 11 at the White House. He said that he wanted literate African Americans and black Union army veterans to have the right to vote in the reconstructed Union, and promised a "new announcement to the people of the South." "That means nigger citizenship," muttered a member of the crowd, the actor John Wilkes Booth. "Now, by God, I'll put him through. That is the last speech he will ever make."[64]

A native of Maryland and an unstable egotist who supported the Confederacy and hated Lincoln, Booth headed a shadowy conspiracy with links to the Confederate secret service, which had intended to kidnap Lincoln and hold him hostage in Richmond. The fall of the Confederate capital ruined that plot, so Booth decided to kill the president. While the Lincolns watched a comedy at Ford's Theatre in Washington on April 14, Booth gained entrance to their box and shot Lincoln in the head. The sixteenth president died at 7:22 the next morning.

Scorned and ridiculed by many critics during his presidency, Lincoln became a martyr and almost a saint after his death. His words and deeds lived after him, and will be revered as long as there is a United States. Indeed, it seems quite likely that without his determined leadership the *United* States would have ceased to be. Union victory in the Civil War resolved two fundamental, festering problems that had been left unresolved by the Revolution of 1776 and the Constitution of 1787. The first problem was the survival of the republic as one nation, indivisible. The republic established by the Founders was a fragile experiment in a world bestrode by kings, queens, emperors, czars, dictators, and theories of aristocracy. Americans were painfully aware that most republics through history had eventually collapsed, degenerated into tyranny, or were overthrown. Some Americans alive in 1861 had seen two French republics rise and fall, several European nationalist republics spring up in 1848 and succumb to counterrevolutions, and republics in Latin America come and go with bewildering rapidity.

In this context of reaction and counterrevolution, Lincoln said in 1862 that the United States represented the "last best, hope" for the survival of republican liberty.[65] The cleavage of the nation in two by the success of the Confederacy would destroy that hope. It would set a fatal precedent by which the minority might secede from the Union whenever it did not like what the majority stood for, until the United States fragmented into a multitude of petty squabbling autocracies. "This issue embraces more than the fate of these United States," Lincoln had said in 1861. "It presents to the whole family of man, the question, whether a constitutional republic, or a democracy— a government of the people, by the same people—can, or cannot, maintain its territorial integrity."[66] Union victory in the Civil War resolved that question. The republic not only survived; in subsequent decades it also grew and prospered and emerged in the twentieth century as the world's arsenal of democracy. Had it not been for Lincoln, this might never have happened.

The second problem left unresolved by the events of 1776 and 1787 was the issue of slavery. By the second quarter of the nineteenth century, a nation founded on a charter that declared all people deserving of the inalienable right of liberty had become the largest slaveholding nation in the world. This was the "monstrous injustice" that made the United States a monument of hypocrisy in the eyes of the world, as Lincoln had expressed it in 1854. With the Emancipation Proclamation, Lincoln started the United States on the road to living up to its professed belief that all men are truly created equal.

More than twenty years earlier, a depressed Lincoln had told Joshua Speed that he would be "more than willing to die" except "that he had done nothing to make any human being remember that he had lived." On New Year's Day in 1863, the Lincolns held a traditional reception in the White House where the president stood for three hours shaking hands with hundreds of people. Exhausted, he retired to his office with a few colleagues to sign the engrossed copy of the Emancipation Proclamation. His hand was so sore from its three hours of social duty that he could scarcely hold the pen. Lincoln did not want to sign while his hand was still trembling, because "all who examine the document hereafter will say 'He hesitated.'" That would not do, for "I never in my life felt more certain that I was doing right than I do in signing this paper. . . . If my name ever goes into history it will be for this act, and my whole soul is in it." Lincoln then picked up the pen and signed his name without a tremor. "That will do," he said.[67]

More than any other American, Lincoln's name has gone into history. He gave all Americans, indeed all people everywhere, reason to remember that he had lived.

Notes

1. Roy P. Basler, ed., *The Collected Works of Abraham Lincoln*, 9 vols. (New Brunswick, N.J., 1953–55), 2:97. Hereinafter CWOL.

2. Ibid., 320.

3. Ibid., 1:509–10.

4. Ibid., 74–75.

5. Ibid., 282.

6. Ibid., 229.

7. *Herndon's Life of Lincoln*, ed. Paul M. Angle (New York, 1949), 304; Joshua Speed to William H. Herndon, Feb. 7, 1866, in *Herndon's Informants: Letters, Interviews, and Statements about Abraham Lincoln*, eds. Douglas L. Wilson and Rodney O. Davis (Urbana, Ill., 1998), 197.

8. CWOL, 1:282.

9. Jason Emerson, *The Madness of Mary Lincoln* (Carbondale, Ill., 2007).

10. *Herndon's Life of Lincoln*, 270.

11. Quoted in Benjamin P. Thomas, *Abraham Lincoln: A Biography* (New York, 1952), 120.

12. Waldo W. Braden, *Abraham Lincoln: Public Speaker* (Baton Rouge, La., 1988), 35–36.

13. CWOL, 2:274.

14. Ibid., 4:67.

15. Ibid., 2:247–83.

16. Ibid., 461.

17. Ibid., 3:9–10.

18. Ibid., 145.

19. Ibid., 2:501, 3:16.

20. Ibid., 3:315, 2:92–93.

21. Ibid., 4:45.

22. Quoted in Harold Holzer, *Lincoln at Cooper Union: The Speech That Made Abraham Lincoln President* (New York, 2004), 113.

23. CWOL, 3:550.

24. Ibid., 4:24–25, 3:478. For the free-labor ideology, see Eric Foner, *Free Soil, Free Labor, Free Men: The Ideology of the Republican Party Before the Civil War* (New York, 1970).

25. CWOL, 4:132–33, 135.

26. Ibid., 160.

27. Ibid., 150, 154, 172.

28. Ibid., 190.

29. Ibid., 262–71.

30. Quoted in James G. Randall, *Lincoln the President*, 4 vols. (New York, 1945–55), 1:326.

31. CWOL, 4:423.

32. *Inside Lincoln's White House: The Complete Civil War Diary of John Hay*, eds. Michael Burlingame and John R. Turner Ettlinger (Carbondale, Ill., 1997), 20.

33. CWOL, 4:268, 7:23, 8:151.

34. Ibid., 5:185.

35. Ibid., 292.

36. *War of the Rebellion . . . Official Records of the Union and Confederate Armies*, 128 vols. (Washington, D.C. 1880–1901), series I, vol. 16, part 2:627. Hereinafter O.R.

37. William F. Smith, *The Francis Preston Blair Family in Politics*, 2 vols. (New York, 1933), 2:144.

38. CWOL, 6:38.

39. *Papers of Ulysses S. Grant*, 29 vols. so far, ed. John Y. Simon (Carbondale, Ill., 1967–), 7:317.

40. *Recollected Words of Abraham Lincoln*, eds. Don E. Fehrenbacher and Virginia Fehrenbacher (Stanford, Calif., 1996), 292.

41. CWOL, 7:324.

42. Ibid., 5:98.

43. *Inside Lincoln's White House*, 193.

44. Edward L. Pierce, *Memoir and Letters of Charles Sumner*, 4 vols. (Boston, 1877–93), 4:114.

45. *Ex parte Merryman*, 17 Fed. Cas. 144.

46. CWOL, 5:421.

47. Ibid., 6:263, 266–67.

48. Ibid., 3:92, 7:281.

49. Ibid., 4:532.

50. Ibid., 5:388–89.

51. Gideon Welles, "The History of Emancipation," *The Galaxy*, 14 (1872), 842–43.

52. CWOL, 5:433–36.

53. Ibid., 6:408–10.

54. Ibid., 7:281; Francis B. Carpenter, *Six Months at the White House with Abraham Lincoln* (New York, 1866), 76–77.

55. Lincoln Papers, Library of Congress.

56. CWOL, 7:451.

57. Ibid., 7:500, 506–7.

58. Ibid., 7:514.

59. Edward McPherson, *The Political History of the United States During the Great Rebellion*, 2nd ed. (Washington, D.C., 1865), 419–20.

60. *O.R.*, series I, vol. 38, part 5:577.

61. CWOL, 8:333.

62. David D. Porter, *Incidents and Anecdotes of the Civil War* (New York, 1885), 294.

63. Ibid., 295; T. Morris Chester's dispatches to the *Philadelphia Press*, in that newspaper April 11, 12, 1865.

64. CWOL, 8:399–405; "Impeachment of the President," *House Report* #7, 40th Congress, 1st Session (1867), 674, quoted in William Hanchett, *The Lincoln Murder Conspiracies* (Urbana, Ill., 1983), 37.

65. CWOL, 5:537.

66. Ibid., 4:426.

67. Several contemporaries described this historic occasion. This account and Lincoln's words are from Frederick W. Seward, *Seward at Washington, as Senator and Secretary of State: A Memoir of His Life, with Selections from His Letters, 1861–1872* (New York, 1891), 151, and from Carpenter, *Six Months at the White House*, 87, 269–70.

Bibliography

The principal collection of Lincoln's papers is the Robert Todd Lincoln Collection in the Library of Congress. Most of the 18,000 items in this collection are incoming letters. The fullest collection of Lincoln's own letters, speeches, and other writings is *The Collected Works of Abraham Lincoln*, ed. Roy P. Basler (8 vols. and an index, 1953–55), with the addition of *The Collected Works of Abraham Lincoln: Supplement 1832–1865*), ed. Basler (1974). The most important of Lincoln's letters and other writings have been selected by Don E. Fehrenbacher and published in two volumes titled *Abraham Lincoln: Speeches and Writings* (1989). Fehrenbacher and his wife, Virginia Fehrenbacher, have co-edited an anthology of Lincoln quotations recalled by hundreds of people who spoke with him titled *Recollected Words of Abraham Lincoln* (1996). A valuable selection of Lincoln writings is *Lincoln on Democracy*, ed. Mario M. Cuomo and Harold Holzer (1990), which has been translated into several languages.

The number of biographies and other books about Lincoln is huge—far greater than for any other figure in American history. Only a selection of the most important can be mentioned here. Lincoln's law partner William Herndon spent several years after Lincoln's death interviewing and corresponding with people who had known him, and gathering other material about the first fifty years of Lincoln's life. This material has been published in *Herndon's Informants: Letters, Interviews, and Statements about Abraham Lincoln*, eds. Douglas L. Wilson and Rodney O. Davis (1998). Herndon collaborated with Jesse W. Weik to present this material in *Herndon's Lincoln: The True Story of a Great Life*, 3 vols. (1889), which has been reprinted in whole or in part in many subsequent editions, of which the best and most recent is *Herndon's Lincoln*, eds. Douglas L. Wilson and Rodney O. Davis (2006). Herndon's account distorted some aspects of Lincoln's life and accepted as true some information that may have been apocryphal. Nevertheless, all subsequent biographers were indebted to Herndon for most of what we know about Lincoln's early life. A year after the appearance of *Herndon's Lincoln*, Lincoln's wartime private secretaries, John G. Nicolay and John Hay, published a ten-volume biography, *Abraham Lincoln: A*

History, which focused mainly on the presidential years. It was the only biography before the second half of the twentieth century to draw on the main collection of Lincoln's papers, which were not opened to the public until 1947.

Before 1947, however, other important biographies appeared, including Lord Charnwood, *Abraham Lincoln* (1917), which was notable for its sympathetic British perspective; Albert J. Beveridge, *Abraham Lincoln 1809–1858*, 2 vols. (1928), whose author died before he could continue the biography into the war years; and Carl Sandburg, *Abraham Lincoln: The Prairie Years*, 2 vols. (1926) and *Abraham Lincoln: The War Years*, 4 vols. (1939), a powerful evocation of Lincoln and his times, which, however, piles up dubious as well as authentic evidence in a mixed profusion. The fullest scholarly biography to appear before 2009, part of it written after the Lincoln papers were opened, is James G. Randall, *Lincoln the President*, 4 vols. (1945–55), with the fourth volume completed after Randall's death by Richard N. Current, who has also written a volume of incisive essays, *The Lincoln Nobody Knows* (1958). Randall's interpretation is marred by a tendency to squeeze Lincoln into a conservative mold that fails to appreciate the depth of his antislavery convictions. The same fault is shared in part by Benjamin Thomas's one-volume biography *Abraham Lincoln* (1952), but is corrected by two other readable biographies: Stephen B. Oates, *With Malice toward None: The Life of Abraham Lincoln* (1977) and Richard Striner, *Father Abraham: Lincoln's Relentless Struggle to End Slavery* (2006). The fullest biography within the covers of a single volume is David Herbert Donald, *Lincoln* (1995). Richard Carwardine, *Lincoln* (2003) provides the perspective of another British scholar who emphasizes the moral dimensions of Lincoln's use of power. Two excellent brief biographies are William E. Gienapp, *Abraham Lincoln and Civil War America* (2002) and Mark E. Neely, Jr., *The Last Best Hope of Earth: Abraham Lincoln and the Promise of America* (1993). Neely has also written a comprehensive and valuable reference work, *The Abraham Lincoln Encyclopedia* (1982), as well as *The Fate of Liberty: Abraham Lincoln and Civil Liberties* (1991).

Several additional biographies and other studies of Lincoln are scheduled to appear during the bicentennial commemoration of his birth in 2009, including a three-volume biography by Michael Burlingame, which will include much new material, and a perceptive one-volume biography by Ronald C. White.

Other studies of specific aspects of Lincoln's life and career include: Gabor Boritt, *Lincoln and the Economics of the American Dream* (1978); Michael Burlingame, *The Inner World of Abraham Lincoln* (1994); LaWanda Cox, *Lincoln and Black Freedom* (1981); Don E. Fehrenbacher,

Lincoln in Text and Context: Collected Essays (1987); Doris Kearns Goodwin, *Team of Rivals: The Political Genius of Abraham Lincoln* (2005); Allen C. Guelzo, *Abraham Lincoln: Redeemer President* (1999) and *Lincoln's Emancipation Proclamation: The End of Slavery in America* (2004); James M. McPherson, *Abraham Lincoln and the Second American Revolution* (1991) and *Tried by War: Abraham Lincoln as Commander in Chief* (2008); William Lee Miller, *President Lincoln: The Duty of a Statesman* (2008); Phillip Shaw Paludan, *The Presidency of Abraham Lincoln* (1994); Ronald C. White, *The Eloquent President: A Portrait of Lincoln Through His Words* (2005); T. Harry Williams, *Lincoln and His Generals* (1952); and Douglas L. Wilson, *Honor's Voice: The Transformation of Abraham Lincoln* (1998) and *Lincoln's Sword: The Presidency and the Power of Words* (2006).

Other Books by James M. McPherson

This Mighty Scourge: Perspectives on the Civil War
Tried by War: Abraham Lincoln as Commander in Chief
Crossroads of Freedom: Antietam
For Cause and Comrades: Why Men Fought in the Civil War
Battle Cry of Freedom: The Civil War Era
Ordeal by Fire: The Civil War and Reconstruction